Words from the Other Woman

THE TRUE ACCOUNT OF A REDEEMED ADULTERESS

Rebecca Halton

with editorial support from Meghan Bardwell

WESTBOW
PRESS
A DIVISION OF THOMAS NELSON

WestBow Press books may be ordered through booksellers or by contacting:

WestBow Press
A Division of Thomas Nelson
1663 Liberty Drive
Bloomington, IN 47403
www.westbowpress.com
1-(866) 928-1240

Because of the dynamic nature of the Internet, any Web addresses or
links contained in this book may have changed since publication and
may no longer be valid. The views expressed in this work are solely those
of the author and do not necessarily reflect the views of the publisher,
and the publisher hereby disclaims any responsibility for them.

Any people depicted in stock imagery provided by Thinkstock are models,
and such images are being used for illustrative purposes only.

Certain stock imagery © Thinkstock.

ISBN: 978-1-4497-1076-7 (sc)
ISBN: 978-1-4497-1078-1 (e)

Library of Congress Control Number: 2010943041

Printed in the United States of America

WestBow Press rev. date: 02/18/2011

*Thank you, **Father God***, for rescuing and redeeming me from my sins, and for sending Your only Son to die so we all could have eternal and abundant life. Your grace never ceases to amaze me.
I love you, Lord.

*Thank you, **Mom & Dad***, for all the sacrifices you have lovingly made over the years, on my behalf. I know you always had the best in mind for me. I love you.

*Thank you, **Lex***, for your fellowship, accountability, and sisterhood. Thank you for believing in me and lovingly encouraging me to answer God's calling by writing this. I love you.

Contents

Introduction

When I was a little girl, I dreamed of what I could become when I grew up. I dreamed of becoming a marine biologist, a wife and mom—even an FBI agent. I can honestly say I did not dream of becoming an adulteress; I'm not sure any of us ever do.

An adulteress, though, is precisely what I was for roughly six months in my early twenties (I say "roughly" because it's not like I marked start and end dates on my calendar). It is a time in my life I look back on now as being the most difficult and pivotal to date. What you are about to read is the story of my relationship with a married man. More importantly, though, it is the story of how I fell from grace, and then how grace saved me.

My prayer, as you begin to venture with me back into this part of my past, is that you are open to what God is communicating through my words to your heart. I pray also that you easily glean wisdom for yourself from lessons I've learned the hard way.

I will tell you now that this book is not a tell-all, but it is my best attempt to honestly look at the relationship I was in. I have made an intentional effort to speak candidly but compassionately. And I have tried to provide explanations for my actions, not make excuses.

There will be points where I speak vaguely and even leave out details you may want. This is intentional, in order to protect innocent people directly or indirectly involved. This may frustrate you, but please bear with me: I truly believe there are some things better left unsaid. The life lessons are still there, even if some of the details are not. For example, I don't think you *need* to know his name in order learn from what I went through.

Ultimately, my deepest desire in sharing this, is to help other people understand a bit more of what adultery looked like from my perspective as "the other woman." By no means do I want to hurt *anyone* by sharing this part of my life in this way; nor is my experience the same as every other person's. The truth is, there is nothing glamorous about being in an affair, but there is everything *glorious* about how God can work in and through one—once we've surrendered to Him.

I will also tell you now that I am not a theologian, nor a Bible scholar, so this book also is not a doctrinal dissection of adultery. I am simply a woman with a heart for telling my story, hoping it will help other people avoid the pain I've experienced myself. I am a child of the Creator of the Universe (as are you), whom He mercifully saved from a deeper plunge into deadly sin. I am a former "other woman." I am a redeemed adulteress. And if, as you're reading this, you are where I was, I'm excited to say that you can find redemption, too. There is hope.

So, take a few deep breaths; pause and pray. Ask that God would open your eyes and heart to what you can learn from what we are about to walk back through together. And learn from what I survived only by God's grace.

1

One of "Those" Girls

I still remember sitting on the floor of my shower, clutching my knees to my chest. I alternated between bowing my head (as though I was trying to hide from God), and leaning my head against the side of the shower (searching the ceiling, as though I was looking for Him). Within minutes, I was crying so hard I lost control of my breathing and started to hyperventilate. It was as if I wanted to exhale as much confusion and pain as possible, with every erratic gasp of air that I gulped in and spewed out.

My tears mixed with the water that flowed from the showerhead above. Deep down, I knew the water that washed over me couldn't *really* cleanse me, but I sat there anyway, even after the hot water turned cold. Among the thoughts that I wanted the water to drown out was the question I had been asking myself often during the previous weeks: *How did I get here?*

"Here" was an adulterous relationship with a married man.

...

I was attracted to him the first time I saw him. There was something about him that instantly made me sit up a little taller, and my heart beat a little faster. He was tall, handsome, and seemed so confident, just by the way he carried himself. (I was usually attracted to confident men because, truth is, I was insecure.)

And then I met his wife.

It then felt as though that same giddy, faster-beating heart had stalled and fallen all the way into the soles of my feet. I felt disappointed, but did not feel like my new mission in life was to seduce him into an extramarital relationship with me.

During the weeks that followed our first meeting, our paths did cross on a predetermined basis, because of the circumstances under which we met. (I realize I'm being vague, and very purposefully so.) I did nothing to avoid these situations where I knew I would most likely see him and his wife. And so, we all began to see each other consistently, and I became better acquainted with him and his wife. I became even more attracted to him as we discovered a comfort and connection with one another that felt very natural.

I soon realized, by what he would say and the ways he would act, that he was also attracted to me. Knowing about his attraction made it harder to deny my feelings for him. And yet I stood and stayed in denial. I should have run in the opposite direction of where this situation was heading—and heading faster than I could have forecasted at the time. Instead, I tried to conceal how I felt from him, his wife, anyone else who observed the two of us interacting—and myself.

When we were around each other, he would joke and tease and flirt. He reminded me of the schoolboys who used to chase me around the playground in elementary school—you know, the ones who like you but don't quite want you to know they like you. He would even say flirtatious things to me in front of his wife. Usually, she would react indifferently or even join in with her own jokes. I can't help but think that her reaction must have been a façade. She must have felt wounded, but didn't want to appear insecure or jealous. (I want to pause here for a moment and encourage wives reading this: you have every right to protect your marriage!)

Despite my growing enjoyment of his attention, I still feigned disgust or disinterest. I did so partly out of denial, and partly out of wanting to protect myself from any suspicion. Up to that point, whenever I saw him was also when I saw her. I wish I could say I was also trying to protect her in some way, but I don't think I was being that noble; I started to like the attention from him too much.

I knew I *shouldn't* like his attention, though. I knew it was wrong to want his attention, which I did. I started to shock myself. *I'm not one of "those" girls*, I thought. *I grew up in a Christian home, with prayers before dinner and special dresses for Sundays; I was christened as a baby and asked Jesus into my heart as a child; I even graduated last summer from a distinguished Christian college. I'm a good girl. I don't do stuff like flirt or date—or more—with someone's husband.*

Truthfully, I was also a very judgmental girl who looked down on women who, intentionally or not, wound up with married men—be it on a few dates, in a relationship, or in bed for one tryst. *I could* never *do that to another woman*, I used to think proudly. *I'm better and smarter than that.*

I knew I wasn't supposed to feel attracted to him, but I didn't know what to do with the feelings I was still having. Looking back now, I see how unwisely I thought that I alone would be stronger and smarter than the temptation creeping in around me. My pride indeed came before my fall.

He attributed her indifference (and his freedom to flirt, even in her company) to the state of their marriage. When he privately detailed for me the trajectory of their relationship, he explained it as a union more out of convenience and platonic partnership than love. And he assured me that she didn't mind his flirtations, as long as she didn't know the details of what he chose to do outside of their marriage.

But no matter how he justified his flirting, it didn't justify my sinful response to his flirting. It didn't matter *why* they got married. What mattered was they did, period. Despite the uneasiness I felt with his reasoning, I gradually guarded my heart less and less around him as I felt more emotionally connected to him. Not guarding my heart with clear boundaries was one of my first mistakes.

Thinking I wasn't capable of making some of the choices I made was another one of my first mistakes. Do not underestimate how powerful temptation can be, especially when you are relying on your own strength to resist it. I thought I was better and smarter than choosing to commit adultery. I thought I could resist the growing temptation without God's help.

It was as though I was standing at the base of a mountain, seeing a crack in the snow at the summit, and thinking that it's not a big problem, that I didn't need to get out of the way. And then the situation grew to where I remained at the base of that mountain as the crack in the snow deepened, the wall of ice and snow began to quake, and I still thought I could stop it from crashing down on me. And if it did fall, I thought I'd survive the impact of the avalanche unfolding right before my eyes.

The Bible says your heart is your wellspring, and Satan is all too happy to try and pollute it because he knows that every action flows from the heart. He will gladly oblige by taking the inch you give him and running with it—not for miles, but until you're dead, destroyed, or pleading for mercy. For your sake I hope it's God's mercy for which you plead.

It's amazing how Satan can influence our thoughts and emotions until we find ourselves rationalizing our sin. Even without the influence of evil, we are fallen human beings with free will. We are capable of making sinful decisions on our own, with little prompting from the enemy and his principalities. We are capable of making decisions like entertaining the advances of a married man, and knowingly entering into an adulterous relationship with him. I know I had the will and responsibility to choose differently.

So why didn't I choose differently? Why was I receptive to his blatantly inappropriate behavior? How was it that I so clearly *knew* adultery was wrong but walked into it anyway? How could I even become friends with his wife and *still* betray her by becoming romantically involved with her husband? I can see the red flags now—in hindsight.

Not long before meeting him, I had moved into my own apartment, which I lived in alone. I had no built-in accountability mechanism in the form of a housemate. I also wasn't at all involved in a church. I wasn't part of a community and fellowship of believers who could reinforce truth and provide added accountability. I wasn't seeking God through regular quiet times, times of prayer and study of His Word. And I didn't think I needed any of that.

I didn't think I needed accountability or community. I didn't think I needed God's help and guidance to avoid the mines of sin in the field of life. I seemed to be doing just fine on my own, with my new apartment and a fabulous new job. So, I was complacent *and* proud—a double whammy that widened the bulls-eye on my back as the principalities at play took aim.

Read and re-read these preceding and next paragraphs carefully: I know you may be where I was. I know you may be thinking you could never do what I did. I know you may be thinking you're doing just fine—maybe even great—without God. Please prayerfully reconsider this attitude. I don't want to scare you, but I want to caution you; I want you to remember that a prideful attitude is precisely what I had before I fell.

Most importantly, in the season in my life in which I met him, I wasn't allowing or truly seeking God to meet my need for positive attention, love, and affirmation of my worth. Those three things are exactly what I was craving when I met him. Only, I was dangerously in denial of how starved I actually was.

I could dismiss or joke away his flirting for only so long; inside, I started to crave the feelings his attention evoked. I even liked the feelings of power and validation. There was something very powerful about feeling *so* desirable to someone as to be able to draw his eye and attention from his spouse. (I know now that *real* power is in self-control and the self-confidence that comes from knowing our worth in God, not in man.)

Now, to help you better understand, we need to go back a little farther into my past, and dig a little deeper into the core of who I am. My hope is that if you recognize yourself in this, you'll proactively seek God for help and transformation now, so as to avoid a similar path as the one I took. I see my red flags in hindsight; I hope sharing them here will provide you with foresight.

This wasn't the first time I craved attention from someone other than God. Being a fairly self-aware person, I have a good idea why there's been this pattern in my past. Like many of us women, I don't think I got the positive affirmation at home that is so critical in helping a girl grow into a confident woman. If we don't get it at home, from the males in our immediate environments and social circles, then we learn to look for it elsewhere. I don't want this to be misinterpreted, though. I consider myself very blessed to have the parents I have. In many ways my parents have been exceptionally supportive, positive influences in my life; people whom God continues to use to shape the woman I am and am becoming.

I also want to be clear that I *love* my dad and three older brothers, but as male influences in the shaping of a young woman, they left some key qualities to be desired. My dad, a former Marine (of whom I am *very* proud), was deployed or working a lot while I was younger. He also tends to be more emotionally reserved, and didn't always seem comfortable with communicating that I was beautiful, that he delighted in me, and that I was worth far more than what most guys my age would offer. His personality is different from mine in many ways, and in this way it wasn't right or wrong. He's just different in a way that often made learning my own worth, or where to best look for it, difficult.

Although he has helped shape who I am, I don't blame him for what I did; and as an adult I've learned that we can't fault people for the choices *we* make. I've taken into account, too, that the bulk of his parenting practice (prior to me) was on my brothers. My brothers have had (and still have) levels and types of emotional needs that are different from mine.

So, when little ol' me came along, it was a whole new ball game for my parents. And I don't mean a ball of "sugar and spice and everything nice," either. In fact, I'm pretty sure that at certain points in my life (especially my teenage years), I made U.S. Marine Corps training look like a cakewalk.

My brothers, on the other hand, seemed to delight in doing whatever they could to tease and torment me. To be fair, I cringe while watching *myself* in childhood home movies because of how I behaved or reacted towards them, too (the word "bratty" comes to mind).

A few years ago, I recall one of my brothers humorously telling me I should thank them for helping make me the woman I am today. I see their reasoning, however warped it is, but I think God would have done just fine without all of them being so "helpful." And so, with immediate male role models who couldn't seem to communicate the kinds of healthy, positive affirmation girls specifically need, I tended to take positive attention almost any time it came my way.

Once I started dating as a teenager, positive attention usually came my way in the form of a noncommittal, immature guy who understood lust more than love, and in some cases, was deceitful, unfaithful, and/or verbally abusive. I would usually start out guarded (bracing for the negative criticism I'd become accustomed to through my brothers), but the more positive attention and affection I received from a guy pursuing or dating me, the more I lowered my guard and latched onto that source of feel-good validation.

In time, though, the positive affirmation most of my boyfriends initially offered would wilt; the lust would rust; the infatuation would fade; and I would be left wondering what had gone wrong. Until a certain age, I thought *I* was what had gone wrong. I often felt I was the one most at fault, and made excuses for them that usually involved me not being enough or doing enough to keep their affection.

All that said, I know that I can't change the past or the people in my past, but I know I can change. I can choose to ask God to change my heart, mind, and spirit now, and for the future. I know I am whole in Christ and Christ alone. And I know that God's affirmation is the only affirmation I need.

This doesn't mean I now "have it all together" (although I still try to sometimes). Being imperfect, I don't always walk in the truth. One truth I do try to walk in is that the world's affirmation is not always positive, but God's affirmation is *always* positive. Even when His affirmation feels negative, the truth is His words are still for the purpose of refining me and making me more like Jesus, which is the most positive affirmation of all.

...

And so my adulterous relationship with him began: first with "harmless" flirting, progressing to an "innocent" e-mail or phone call, before advancing to an invitation to "simply" hang out, just the two of us. (Seeing a pattern here?) Before I knew it, I was double-checking my hair before I left the apartment to see him, making sure I smelled and looked especially attractive—all while lying to myself: *we're just friends*. Honestly, I'm not sure I ever was just his friend, considering how I felt that first time I saw him. Meanwhile, Satan and his spiritual thugs worked quickly, while I remained in denial that they were at work at all.

2
The First Kiss

I knew kissing him was wrong. I wonder how many angels were outside the car (or inside it, for that matter), fighting to hold me back, to spare me from that Pandora's Box of a kiss. If I could, I would travel back to my twenty-something self and yank her out of that car (by her hair, if necessary).

We were sitting in his car when it happened. Only, it didn't "just" happen, as if by accident. We were talking, late into the night, and even luring each other into that kiss. I see now how that car was like the forbidden tree in the Garden of Eden. And that kiss was like the apple in the sense that, once tasted, it opened floodgates of emotions that made walking away as easy as swimming to the shore of a whitewater rapid. I was in way over my head.

Conviction immediately followed that kiss. But I still didn't walk away from him entirely. Instead, I began explaining why it wouldn't—couldn't—happen again. Ever. I wrongly thought it would somehow not be as bad if I could say that the kiss happened but I regretted it and it wouldn't ever happen again. After all, I wasn't one of "those" girls. Or was I? I wasn't so sure anymore.

In the days that immediately followed that first kiss, I fretted about how I didn't want to hurt anyone (he assured me I wasn't/wouldn't), and went back and forth between conviction and confusion. I was still attracted to him—more than before. The kiss had introduced physical intimacy into the equation, which compounded the emotional intimacy we had established through conversations that became more and more personal.

And then she called me within a week of the kiss. Inside, I was panicking, but outwardly tried to remain calm. I figured if I could just make it through the phone call, I would completely end it with him as soon as she and I hung up.

I felt even worse—even more disgusted with myself—when I realized that she wasn't calling to cuss me out for having kissed her husband, but to make sure I was okay. She did suspect something—but that something was that I was uncomfortable with some of his joking when we were all together. She said she wanted to make sure I was okay. To this day, I don't know if she knew then what had happened up to that point.

I can't remember exactly how or why, but she then confided in me that they had been trying to have a baby. I was simultaneously sick to my stomach and infuriated. I knew he was out of town, and not with her, so I immediately called his cell phone after talking with her, saying I was done, it was over. I told him I had found out about them trying to have a baby, and I didn't want to hurt anyone. I put my foot down; if only I had kept it there.

He, however, minimized her confession by saying they had tried to have a baby "a while ago." Then he assured me of his interest and the feasibility of our newfound fling. And although I was never fully convinced this could even remotely be a good idea, oddly enough, I found myself justifying the idea just enough so that I could continue seeing him. I had started to experience the euphoric feelings associated with his affection, and I didn't want them to stop (key word: "feelings"). I enjoyed the way I felt around him, and we both agreed it felt effortless to talk and spend time with each other.

I had taken the bait and was now hanging on the hook. Any time I tried to yank myself off, it hurt enough that I'd stop for fear of greater pain that I didn't want to feel. So I stayed, and steadily we fashioned a relationship out of a fling that resulted from a kiss that came weeks after that first look, that first moment of adulterous attraction in our hearts. In a few short weeks, it had spiraled downward that much—I didn't know it then, but we had farther to go. And with each step closer to him, the more deeply I cared about him and the less I felt I could just walk away.

I don't want to mislead you into thinking I was held against my will. I didn't always want to walk away. There were enough wonderful moments with him that enticed me into staying.

It was nice to know he thought of me, and it felt good to get the thoughtful gifts he would give. In the beginning, there was even something that felt exciting and mysterious about meeting in secret, or seeing each other in public and knowing what no one else knew. We would usually meet to have lunch or dinner together. I'd thoughtfully cook something we could eat at my kitchen table for two, where we could pretend (and only pretend) it was just us. Sometimes, we'd meet to curl up on the couch and watch a movie. And yes, the time we spent together usually included physical intimacy that neither of us had any right to have with each other—and for which I've chosen to repent.

Within a week or two of that kiss, he said he loved me. That seems ironic now, because real love doesn't encourage the loved one to disobey God, but to obey Him—because that's how we love God. By obeying our lustful, selfish feelings instead, he and I were disobeying God in a way that I have no doubt broke His heart.

Soon into the relationship, the emotional highs and lows became extreme. One minute I would be giddy with the exhilaration accompanying his affection, the delight of being desired and "in love" with someone who felt like my best friend. The next, I would be gripped with conviction, and haunted by the fear of being found out. As the dishonesty festered within me, I eventually chose to confide in my closest friends and family. I was starting to recognize I needed help.

3

The Intoxication of Infatuation

The intoxication of our infatuation had become like a drug. The emotional highs were just addicting enough that I could bear the lows for only so long before wanting to see or talk to him again. I remember restlessly lying in bed at night, alone, unable to sleep because my mind was too busy wondering what he was doing at that exact moment. I would stare at the ceiling, softly lit by late-night city lights outside my downtown apartment's windows. I would lay there wondering what he was doing, if he was talking with her—even if he was having sex with her—while I was there alone, like the fool I was being.

We would usually talk by phone in the morning, before work. Early into the relationship, those conversations were flirtatious early morning greetings, after not being able to talk with each other the entire night he was at home, and before not being able to talk while I was in the office. Eventually, though, the purpose of those conversations was for me to purge whatever emotions and fear-filled thoughts had built up overnight, and him calming me down. It was draining.

I found out later that yes, while being sexually active with me, he was also still sexually active with her. Maybe they were even still trying to have a baby. My immediate reaction was fear. I was fearful about the increased risks to my health by him having multiple partners (especially not knowing if she felt the same freedom as he did to have relationships outside of their marriage).

And I was upset. I tearfully told him how hurt I felt, because he knew how meaningful it was that I would have any degree of physical intimacy with him. I also felt confused, wondering how could he "love" me, but still have sex with her. But at the same time that I felt crushed, I also felt resigned. After all, it's not like I had any right to be angry that he was having sex with his own wife. I was the other woman, not her.

That pivotal realization was one of several key moments of truth. Each of those moments (more to follow) chipped a few more of the scales from my eyes. Even without those sobering milestones in the relationship, the day-to-day dynamic of sustaining a sinful relationship was tumultuous. The dynamic between us personally wasn't, which was largely why it still felt so difficult to leave.

After all, we "loved" each other, and by the world's standards, he treated me well: he was encouraging and supportive, funny, and loving. He brought me thoughtful gifts and even took me out in public on what he and I knew were dates. I felt valuable to him and comfortable with him, and I liked both of those feelings. The secrecy required in an adulterous relationship also creates a certain, strong bond between the two people involved. But when I was alone, it was another story, especially as my mind would wander down alleys of possibilities I knew could all too quickly become realities—some of them irreversible.

On at least one occasion, I was afraid of becoming pregnant or contracting a sexually transmitted disease. In only one month, I lost twelve pounds, as I also lost more and more of my appetite. Paranoia and anxiety began to consume me to the point that I couldn't stomach consuming much else.

Whenever I would stumble upon an episode of one of those talk shows—the ones that serve up people's painfully poor life choices on silver platters for the public to gnaw on—I used to jest fearfully with him that we were going to end up on one of those shows someday. And if we did, I joked (but not really) that she would probably throw slurs or a chair at me, or pull my hair, or claw me in the face—and I would have felt like I deserved it.

And then there was the article I read about a woman who sued her husband's mistress (and won). Suddenly, visions of subpoenas and private investigators staked outside my apartment started dancing through my scared head. As my mind wandered farther and farther into the frightful realm of possibilities of how this could eventually unravel, I started to feel like I'd just be lucky to get out alive.

After all, adultery that has resulted in the punishment, harassment, harm, *or even death* of at least one of the people involved isn't unheard of. Throughout history, the world has responded to adultery in some atrocious ways. For example, humiliating, disfiguring, maiming and even murdering women who have been accused (correctly or not) of adultery are practices that continue today.

Not to make you think men don't also suffer consequences of adultery, but in many cultures in which adultery has been or is so systematically punished in these ways, women are generally more often the ones targeted. In some places, not centuries ago but to this very day, someone would feel fully justified (and perhaps even glorified by his or her family or community) in physically harming me for what I have confessed in these pages. I can't be afraid though; instead, I trust God and offer His hope.

In the Bible, Jesus demonstrated a very different treatment of the adulteress. I'm thinking of one occasion in particular. A woman caught in adultery was brought to Jesus by a crowd of people. When the crowd—including religious leaders—asked Jesus what should be done with the woman based on a law that allowed for her to be stoned to death, what did Jesus do? Rather than condemn her, *He defended her*. Rather than stand by the crowd, He stood by the outcast (whom He did also tell to *leave her life of sin* after the crowd disbanded).

I won't delve into the entire context (nor do I feel qualified to do it justice), but not only did Jesus defend her, He did so in a very wise and diplomatic way that challenged the crowd, convicting even the most religious among them. He invited anyone who is without sin to throw the first stone at her. No one did, because no one could: they knew they were not without sin. And so it is with us: who of us is without sin?

I have also realized that one of the worst responses societies can have is minimizing the behavior of the people involved in the affair, minimizing the severity of their choices and risks. Please do not misunderstand me. I'm not encouraging physical or figurative stoning, but we can still love someone without loving his or her behavior. I'm still learning how to do this.

But when we behave like it's not a big deal, we are giving an impression of permission, whether we mean to or not. We should lovingly encourage people vulnerable to or involved in an affair to change course—not act like they're not on the spiritual equivalent of a train heading for an overpass with missing tracks. We should all do a better job of protecting and respecting marriage.

Another feeling I often felt while on the roller coaster of this relationship was guilt. The guilt was different from conviction, in that guilt still gave me excuses to stay; conviction urged me to end the sinful behavior. I periodically felt this guilt-based responsibility to use my time with him to counsel him about his marriage; truthfully, I think I was trying to create a "good" reason for him to spend time with me.

I also think part of me thought that if I couldn't walk away from him, I could get him to walk away from me. As deeply drawn as I was to him, I knew in my heart I couldn't keep him; I hadn't forgotten that he wasn't mine to have in the first place. And so, I thought if he was going to spend time with me, maybe I could get him to spend it thinking about her. I would encourage him to invest more in his relationship with her; to consider her feelings more; to believe more in the relationship he could have with her, since he really shouldn't have one with me.

I don't believe for a second that this therapist "hat" I attempted to wear at times made me heroic and considerate, but it does show more of the complicated dynamics and confusion that accompanied this relationship. As often as there were times that I wanted to save him from himself, there were as many times that I wanted to steal him for myself.

No matter what I did, though, within a few months, I finally reached the point of being ready to point him to the door. He had reached a point, too, but a very different one.

4

A Bombshell

I remember the night he told me he was going to divorce her. I had told him the night before that it was over; after three months, I wasn't going to continue the relationship with him. I meant it this time, or meant to mean it.

He called me the next night sounding casual, as if I hadn't just told him twenty-four hours before that the relationship was over. He asked if he could come by my apartment and talk with me. I foolishly said yes. Then, there in my bedroom, as I sat on my bed and he knelt on the floor beside it, looking up at me with hope-filled eyes, he told me he had decided to end it with her. And be with me.

I didn't know what to say—or think—at first. The seriousness of his choice wasn't lost on me. I sat there quietly as his weighty words sank in, and I wondered if it really could work out for us. I had dreamed of us being together—legitimately together—one day. My heart flipped and flopped between wanting him not to leave me and wanting him not to leave her.

He assured me of his feelings for me and explained the need for distance between us temporarily, as he discreetly began exploring options with an attorney. At that point, I felt a sense of responsibility to stay in the relationship, because I had helped bring it to this point. I had helped lead and lure him to this decision, and asked myself: *How can I turn him away now?*

It's not like I hadn't thought of him divorcing her; or thought I wanted him to divorce her; but the thought and the reality are two very different things. On more than one occasion during the relationship, I actually thought it would work out with us if he divorced her. At times, I thought we would miraculously become this wonderful, happy, blended family. She might even thank me someday for being the catalyst that eventually freed her from a relationship in which she wasn't being loved like she deserved. I was delusional. I was deceiving myself.

I knew in my heart it would be extremely difficult to fully trust him, after the way our relationship began. I knew I would struggle to trust him to not do to me what he did to her. I knew that I would be suspicious of who he was calling, e-mailing, or texting—and of whom he was spending his time with when he wasn't with me. And, I almost felt like I would deserve to endure that suspicion if we ultimately ended up together. I saw this relationship with a man I couldn't truly trust as a bed I helped make, and I believed I deserved to lie in it.

What followed his declaration that night were three more months of waiting, of thinking that somehow our "love" would survive and conquer all, as though I were in a Jane Austen novel gone terribly wrong. Somehow, I imagined, the adulteress would be absolved, and all would be made right. His wife would even realize it was for her own good, and we'd all live happily ever after. Yeah, right.

And then something happened that got him thinking twice about his decision to explore divorce. Something I'm not going to detail here (I told you this wouldn't be a tell-all). Besides, the important thing is not what exactly happened but that it happened. And when it did, it chiseled a bunch of those scales from *both* of our eyes. It injected a much-needed dose of reality into the situation, reminding us all that more was at stake than our happiness. It caused us to surface after months of sticking our heads in the sand of selfishness.

(By the way, if you're reading this while in an affair, chances are your own "something" will happen, too. It's only a matter of time; of when and how powerfully the dose of reality will hit one or both of you.)

5

Wake-Up Calls

I knew how my parents would react before I even told them. It was shortly before Christmas when I confessed, and already several weeks into the relationship. I was past the point of thinking it was going to just be a one-time kiss I'd regret but not have to tell anyone about, or a passing fling I could pass off as a momentary lapse in judgment. I was emotionally weary and wanting help, wanting open arms I could run to—arms that weren't his.

Part of me hoped those arms would be my parents', but a bigger part knew not to expect that. I knew where they stood: for them, taking a stance on adultery was as simple and clear-cut as choosing their side of the line in the sand.

Sure enough, they reacted as I expected and not as I hoped. I still remember sitting in my kitchen as I told them over the phone. I can't remember if he was there with me or not. I had most of my difficult conversations with friends and family, without the support of his presence.

I remember hearing the disappointment in my mom's voice. I remember her firmly, calmly telling me that as long as I was in the relationship, I was not welcome in their home—including at Christmas. I wasn't expecting them to roll out the red carpet or anything, but I was also hoping they would have resisted any such ultimatums. I felt not just alone, but ostracized; and by my own parents.

I was hurt, I was confused, but I was also still proud enough that I didn't want to give them the satisfaction of doing what they told me to do (walk away from him). I truly do admire my parents' ability to stand courageously in their convictions, no matter what. And I understand and respect that they didn't want to appear to condone the behavior. I truly believe they thought they were doing what was best.

But through their black-and-white lens, I don't think they saw how simple it *wasn't* for me to just walk away. As I would learn, finally breaking free from the emotional and spiritual entanglements of adultery would require the spiritual equivalent of the Jaws of Life.

Despite having a good sense of what their reaction would be, I told them because I was tired of lying to them. In case you haven't noticed, I can be a pretty transparent person, so harboring this affair from my parents was hard. We don't always see eye to eye, but I try to be straightforward with them, just as they are with me.

I also told them because I wanted help with walking away. I told them because I wanted them to say they loved me no matter what, and that I could come home any time, any hour, and they would be there with open arms. Instead, they didn't, and I turned to the one person I felt I could: him.

Thanksgiving, Christmas, and New Year's all came and went that year, and I spent almost all of them completely alone. I had fantasized feasting over a romantic Thanksgiving dinner for two, opening presents together on (or around) Christmas morning, and ringing in the new year with him by my side. But none of that happened. Instead, I hungrily consumed whatever slivers of time he could spare—spare because his priority was holiday plans he had with his own wife and relatives (and rightly so).

Not everyone reacted as my parents did. I told a close circle of friends, who encouraged me and prayed for me—not because they condoned my behavior (I knew they did not) but because they wanted to help. (I also believe my parents were praying for me.) I can't tell you how many tear-filled phone calls those friends and I had. Many times our conversations would begin with me crying so hard that they would have to wait until my breathing stabilized again before we could resume talking.

I can only imagine what a slap in the face my news felt like to my friends who were already married by then. I got a sense of that when I visited a friend and her husband one weekend. I told them prior to my visit about the relationship, and they still encouraged me to come so we could talk and they could counsel me in person. As we sat around their kitchen table, as they listened to and guided me, my friend broke down. She tearfully told me how painful my actions were for her as a wife.

I think the hardest part about her confession was that she wasn't angry: she was heartbroken. It was another of those wake-up calls I needed. The honesty of her reaction pierced my shield of self-denial; her vulnerability drew me out of my selfish circumstances long enough to see—actually see right in front of me—that I was hurting people I loved. It was one thing to think I was just disappointing people I loved, it was another thing to *know* I was causing them pain.

6
Final Good-bye

The road from that first meeting to the final good-bye was a long, turbulent one. I feel sad for people who stay on the path of adultery for years, even decades, because whether or not they are willing to acknowledge it, their adultery is robbing them of time, energy, emotion, and life they will not be able to reclaim. That's not melodrama: that's reality.

It wasn't easy at first, but I gradually got my footing again. I began going to a local church, even inviting him to go with me. Once again, I thought if we were going to be together, I could at least try to witness... with whatever witness I had left. I also stayed connected to my closest friends, and am convinced their prayers for me were heard and answered graciously.

As I started to draw closer to God again, I also started to see the situation for what it *really* was: sad. I started to see him not as a lover or best friend, but as a sad person in need of something (actually, Someone) far greater than I could ever be to him. The same fruit that had tasted so sweet that night in the car was now tasteless. Not even bitter or sour, just tasteless.

Eventually, he concluded he couldn't divorce her, and I concluded I couldn't stay with him. It ended the best way I can think of: we both walked away. He had often expressed regret that he couldn't give me the relationship I really deserved, and I *finally* reached the point of believing that for myself. During the majority of the relationship, I would tell us both that whatever I got from him was worth far more than what I would get from any other man.

I used to think that the crumbs of his life were far more satisfying than the prime cut of someone else's. What I was really saying is I believed I was worth crumbs and was getting exactly what I deserved, by being the other woman. I wasn't in a position to demand more, although I tried at times on the basis of our "love."

Not for a second do I take for granted that it didn't end another way. The truth is, I could have contracted a sexually transmitted disease or become pregnant, which would have brought a whole new set of life-changing challenges. I could have ended up the second wife of a man I didn't trust (if he had divorced her). I could have ended up embroiled in a bitter divorce proceeding—theirs or our own (if he and I ended up together). I could have ended up dead, seeing as how death is the wages of sin (again, not to be misconstrued as an endorsement of literal or figurative stoning).

Before we permanently parted ways, he did apologize to me for any pain he caused me. I have often wondered if (and hoped that) he has also apologized to her. Even if not in words, through a verbal confession of what happened, then in his actions, by becoming the husband she deserves—a man who is faithful to and grateful for her, and not just for the ways she makes his life more convenient. That would be the best apology of them all.

7

Speaking Out

I can't remember when I first started talking openly about the adultery, but God led me to a point where I stopped being afraid of what people would think about it. I realized that silence pleases Satan, and speaking truth pleases God. Having already sampled the rotten fruits of Satan's handiwork, I decided anything I could do to displease him would be worth doing. More importantly, I realized there is *power* in speaking truth.

So, I started talking and writing about the affair. I started to invite God to work through me in other people's relationships, people I would tell about what He gloriously and graciously has done in my life. My openness has made some people in my life very uncomfortable, temporarily or to this day. But, I truly believe God's glory is more important than their (or my) comfort, so I testify. I choose to let God make something positive out of a negative part of my life.

In addition to the close friends I told while I was in the relationship, I also told significant people after it was over. For example, approximately six to eight months after the affair, I began dating someone else (someone not married). He was (and still is, as far as I know) a *good* man. He was trustworthy, loving, considerate, and consistent. He used to say, "Give me something I can swing at," and that included my adultery. To him the affair was a nonissue. To me, it was as if God communicated through him just how immediately forgiven I was.

That relationship ended for its own reasons, but as I autopsied it, I realized I had brought in unpacked baggage from the affair. There was an afternoon—months after that boyfriend and I broke up—that he and I were talking, and I started crying. I finally understood that I had walked into that relationship with him still deeply wounded from the affair. I realized I hadn't allowed for true healing. I had put a Band-Aid on a wound that needed surgery and stitches instead, and pretended I was emotionally healthier than I actually was.

I also realized that fears and doubts and distrust—all of which reared their ugly heads in that follow-up relationship—had followed me from the affair. I sobbed that afternoon I talked with my ex-boyfriend (true to form, he did his best to listen to and comfort me). I was sad, but also angry. It was then I realized that the affair hadn't just negatively affected one relationship (his marriage), but now two (his marriage and my dating relationship). I wondered how much less damage I would have done in that relationship if the one before it hadn't been so damaging.

After I started sharing about the affair, I realized there is a difference between talking about something and talking about it *truthfully*. In my case, it took me a while after I started talking about it to stop qualifying the relationship. I used to diplomatically clarify for people that, "While we crossed some physical boundaries, others we did not." Where my motive in being vague in this book has been to protect the innocent, my motive in making those qualifications was selfish. I used to qualify it (sometimes in more detail than that), because I wanted to be *very* careful about what other people thought of me. After all, I couldn't have them thinking I was one of "those" girls, could I? Eventually, though, I abandoned that approach. Because the truth is: sin is sin, and if we're not careful, we all have it in us to be one of "those" girls, because we're all human.

Still, even after speaking truthfully about what happened, some people I've told have reacted as though what I've done "isn't that big of a deal." I don't know if they do that to try and make me not feel bad, but try saying "it's not a big deal" to the people I know whose marriages have ended and lives have forever changed because their spouse was having an affair.

Try telling that to the woman about to be literally or figuratively stoned; or the monogamous man who just found out he contracted a sexually transmitted disease from his own wife, who unbeknownst to him was sexually active with someone else. It's a very big deal, and had I remained in the relationship, there is no doubt in my mind it would have only become an even bigger deal in my life.

Sadly, though, to many in our society, adultery doesn't seem like a big deal. Partly because we misunderstand what adultery really is. This misunderstanding has got to change. Or we weigh what happened between two people on a scale of "wrong," and determine if what happened is "not so bad," "bad," or "unforgiveable."

In God's eyes, the adultery that happens first with the eyes and the heart is no less a sin than the adultery that happens with the body. The Bible says a person who has looked lustfully at another person has already committed adultery in his or her heart. People have asked me if he and I had sex, or other questions pertaining to the physical intimacy of our relationship. That's the "spectrum" view of adultery; one that ranks a person's sin, when God is already clear.

When I omit certain details about the physical nature of the affair I was in, it's not because I still feel shame or because I'm trying to be mysterious. I am trying to be wise, but I'm also trying to emphasize that what happened first between his heart and mine was no less sinful in God's eyes than what happened at any point between our bodies.

Our understanding of sin should hinge on God's Word, not on people's judgment of whether or not he and I had a flirtation but not intercourse, or it wasn't adultery until that first kiss. Sin is sin and truth is truth, and acknowledging the sin in your life is the first step to overcoming it. You first have to know the enemy you're dealing with before you can know how to defeat it with God.

So, now it's one of my missions in life to snitch on Satan where he's lurking in and around relationships. I'm stepping into the light and ready to step on some evil toes. I am determined to allow God to use me to foil the enemy's evil plans to crush as many covenant relationships as possible. I want to be a whistle-blower for God, sounding the alarm on Satan's schemes, because even though my story is unique, his tactics are not. He's not that creative; that's why many of the things I've written in these pages have resonated with many of you, too.

He doesn't like my mission, not one bit. Which actually brings me a lot of joy. If there are any three things I've learned from this experience, they're these simple truths: (1) anything that makes Satan mad is worth doing, (2) anything that makes God glad is worth doing, and (3) I cannot gauge what is worth doing by what makes *me* mad or glad.

One thing that makes God glad is forgiveness. I have forgiven the man with whom I was in that relationship, just as God has forgiven me. While reading this, there may have been points when you thought he was a jerk or a weasel. He's no more one than you or I can be. He is a man, a fallen human being just like you and me.

He and I both made our share of wrong choices, and neither of us can neglect the responsibility and opportunity we each had to make different choices. We can't change that now, but my hope is that the experience—in some way—has taught him even half as much as it's taught me. It's not my responsibility to make sure that happens, though, so I've maintained my distance since we said our last good-bye more than two and a half years ago.

I used to think about confessing to his wife and asking her for forgiveness, acknowledging my role and responsibility and telling her how sorry I am for any pain my actions caused her. I don't know how much she knew or knows, though, and, right or wrong, I haven't volunteered that confession to her. My confession is mine to make, but his is not. And telling her would require confessing for him, too.

I think if I had told her, it would have been more for my own peace of mind than hers. It would have been more for me to feel like a good person than to do what was good for the situation. And what seemed like good for the situation is what I've done by backing out (and staying out) of their lives, praying that God would be glorified and their relationship transformed. If I am ever in a position to ask for her forgiveness I will—while standing in the confidence of knowing that whether she chooses to or not, God already has forgiven me.

8

Redemption

*T*here is one simple reason I'm able to talk about the relationship now: redemption as a result of God's grace, which is available to us because Jesus Christ died for our sins and rose again. In fact, redemption is why I *like* talking about the relationship now.

Please don't misunderstand me: I'm not proud of my behavior and sinful choices. But, I do like to boast in what God did—and continues to do—through that experience in my life. It was easily the most formative experience of my faith so far.

I went from piously thinking so highly of myself that I would judge and condemn other adulterous women, to knowing how fallen I am outside of God's grace and love. It's very humbling. And experiencing the consequences of trying to operate outside of obedience to Him is one of the hardest—but best—life lessons I have learned. Having learned it the hard way, I now try to spare myself some more hard knocks by staying closer to Him, and in greater obedience to His will and commands. (It may not feel like it if you're not there right now, but the closer you are to Him, the freer, not more confined, you are.)

It's been more than two and a half years since I've been in any kind of contact with him. I blocked his e-mail address and changed my phone number; I've also moved to another state, but not specifically to evade him. It just happened that by God's grace, He has led me to a new place. That doesn't mean the affair's been erased from my mind, though.

You can forgive and be forgiven, but I don't think you should forget. You shouldn't dwell on it; you should ask God for healing and walk in the freedom of knowing you have been forgiven, but you shouldn't forget the risks and red flags and the reasons you would never go down a particular road again.

For me, not forgetting has meant remembering the importance of boundaries in relationships, romantic or not. It's also meant remembering how eagerly and "innocently" Satan will work to destroy you. Finally, it's meant never—*never*—forgetting how incredibly God plucked me out of the relationship and restored me, once I was ready to take hold of the open hand He was extending to me the whole time.

At times, I have wondered if I deserve to have happen to me what I have done to someone else. I have even caught myself emotionally bracing for it, as if it is inevitable that I will marry one day, and my husband will cheat on me. God's answer to that is a decisive, resounding "No." I wouldn't deserve it. That's not what repentance and redemption are, nor is it how grace and mercy work—karma, maybe. If it were how God's grace and mercy worked, we'd all be in trouble.

When I repented, when I sought God's forgiveness and turned away from the relationship, I took the key that God offers each and every one of us, and unshackled the chains of guilt and shame weighing down my life. He could have stopped there. God could have just spared me from any additional pain and consequence beyond what I had already endured. Instead, He went above and beyond by restoring what was broken during or because of the adultery.

He didn't have to restore my relationship with my parents, but He did. Eventually, I was welcomed back into their home, and was even able to discuss more about what happened. I also spent the following Christmas with them, and in fact wrote portions of this book while visiting them.

God also didn't have to reconcile my best friend and me. My adultery caused a deep divide between us; it created division, but not silence, as she continued to pray for me. But He did reconcile us, and now I am not only "Auntie Bec" to her son but godmother to her firstborn daughter.

Perhaps most beautifully, He did not have to spare me from irreversible consequences of my actions, didn't have to preserve me physically and restore me emotionally for marriage, but He did. I have since recommitted myself to abstinence prior to marriage, and now look forward to marriage with a deeper appreciation and respect for it *because* of what happened. I now look forward to one day being face to face with my husband…*almost* as much as I look forward to one day being face to face with my Father in heaven who saved me.

I am also more keenly aware of how cunningly Satan can work to destroy covenant relationships, be it by marring an existing marriage or tainting someone's future spouse in advance of that covenant. Because of my experience, I am surer than ever of why I need to depend on God for wisdom, protection, mercy, grace, and love. And what an incredible love it is. Not only has He redeemed me, He has also blessed me, even when He had every right and reason not to.

I do expect there will still be at least one conversation my future husband and I will have about the affair.

Whatever peace I can provide him I will, and I know that with the Holy Spirit as our mediator, we will be able to communicate truthfully and lovingly, and God will be glorified. Should God choose to bless us with children, there will also be conversations I will honestly have with my children (once they're old enough)—for the glory of God and for their benefit.

I admit, though: some days it's still a struggle to not feel distrustful of men, or to brace myself for some sort of backlash. I travel regularly, and there's something about airports that makes me feel like I'm going to run into him again in one. But I know God is with me, leading me through these remaining steps towards complete healing.

And my heart breaks every time a friend or acquaintance reveals their marriage or the marriage of someone they care about has suffered from adultery. I emotionally try to prepare myself for whatever reaction they may have when I tell them I was once the other woman. I brace myself to bear the words or emotions they are not at liberty to unleash on the woman who has interfered or is interfering with the marriage they've mentioned. For the most part, though, they've calmly sought advice instead. Still, I ask God to thicken my skin as much as is needed to bear whatever blows are administered in the name of their healing.

9

From Me to You

Moving on from the affair was essential, but it wasn't always easy. I will say, though, that by God's grace, I have been able to move forward. Not once did I think to try and reconcile with him and rekindle the relationship. I don't want to go back, especially knowing that I have so much more to look forward to in the future, including my own husband.

So where are you as you're reading this? Regardless of where exactly, there is something for you within this testimony, and I hope you've learned from it. In fact, that—as I mentioned up front—is my greatest hope. I urge you to take away anything positive that you can apply to your life. You, my sister, are worth so much more than what an affair provides—and doesn't provide—you.

So, if you're in one, leave it; and if you're not in one, avoid it at all costs. I can't emphasize this enough: be proactive and vigilant in protecting your relationship.

If you're single and God hasn't called you to a lifetime of singleness, my specific hope is that this testimony has reinforced for you the importance of waiting for your spouse. And I hope it has given you glimpses into how important it is to guard your heart. That, however, is no less important after you've married.

If you're married, my specific hope is that you have seen through my experience how important it is to protect your marriage. You must be proactive. You must be receptive to what your spouse needs, as well as honest about your needs. The adultery I was involved in transpired gradually, not suddenly. He and I didn't wake up one morning in this full-blown affair with a possible divorce.

That's why I advocate for Christ-centered relationships and boundaries in co-ed friendships before and after marriage, to help guard each person's heart and preserve them for their spouse. Not that everyone gets married, but given the odds that most people do, there is a really good chance at least one of you in the friendship will.

And yes, I even believe that men and women—heterosexual men and women—cannot be just friends, not without boundaries and the inclusion of third parties, especially if one of those third parties is a spouse or future spouse. At some point, at least one of the friends will develop and harbor (if not also act on) romantic feelings. Or, at some point, when one of the two people in the friendship is at a vulnerable point in his or her relationship, and leans on the opposite-sex friend for support...well, it's a slippery slope not worth attempting. Plus, there's no advice or support that I *must* get from a male friend that I can't get from my Father in heaven, or from my female friends, or (eventually) from my husband.

This isn't to say I'm perfect now and have all the answers. In fact, on a recent work trip, I was spending some downtime with a male colleague. Since the hotel was our home away from home, the natural place to hang out was in one of our rooms. That's where we ended up hanging out. We enjoyed a couple hours of quiet: he softly played his acoustic guitar; we read classic short stories aloud and attempted s'mores in the microwave.

Nothing physically happened between us, but I knew the emotional ice on which I was walking was thinning as I started thinking about all his attractive attributes. (Not to mention Satan didn't need something to actually happen, in order to influence how others thought of and reacted to finding out we spent time alone in his hotel room.) I went back to my room that night feeling leery. I knew what I should do, even though he and I were both single and technically "free" to spend that kind of time together as friends.

The following morning, I told him we should look for public places to hang out (or the company of others) in the future. Those are the kinds of boundaries that may sound old-fashioned, but they are the kinds of boundaries that will help protect you and your heart until the time and person are right. Ask yourself what you're truly willing to risk, and at what cost: an evening of fun, or your heart. For your sake, I hope you will not be shortsighted and see only so far as the moment you're in.

I've already specifically spoken to single and married women, but now I want to talk to the adulteresses who are reading this. There are two types of adulteresses to whom I want to speak: the type who is remorseful and ready to find a way out of the relationship, and the type who has no moral qualms about starting and staying in the relationship. I'm not oblivious to the fact that some women are okay with the idea of being in a relationship with someone who is married.

First, to the women who think they are fine in their adulterous relationship, I know my battle is not with you but with the principalities playing your heart like a harp. I pray you are awakened to the presence of those principalities in your life and relationship. You are playing with fire, my friend. And you *will* be burned by it; it's not a question of if but when. And a question of how—such as an unplanned pregnancy; a life-threatening, sexually transmitted disease; emotional trauma, such as a broken heart if he reaches the point of wanting out first; or worse. I realize my case, and how neatly it concluded, is likely more the exception to the rule than the rule itself. That is something to consider, and consider seriously.

But for you my heart also breaks. You are worth far more than what he can give you, no matter how much he may say he wants to give you more. There are opportunities in life that you will miss because of the choices you're making now. That's just the reality of life, and while God offers His grace and redemption every day we are alive, each day is all we have—and have only once.

I don't have to know you personally to know that I want the best for you, and to know that the only true way to receive the best for your life is through God by way of His amazing Son, Jesus Christ. I previously said that I eventually realized that escaping the entanglements of my affair would require the spiritual equivalent of the Jaws of Life. Well, that's Jesus—only He is the Bread of Life that miraculously saves us from the jaws of death. Jaws that are wide and open around you right now; jaws that I hope you ask for His help in escaping before it's too late.

Now, for the women who are ready to get out, my specific hope for you is that you know and receive God's love for you. That you would know how meticulously and beautifully He made you. Leaving is a tough—but brave and important—step that I encourage you to take.

I still remember the thoughts and feelings that went through my mind and heart, and so I can relate to where you're at right now. Hoping for the happily-ever-after best with your married man, while on the other hand wanting to just walk away. I know the feelings, and I even went into some of those online "support" forums to have those feelings validated by other women in similar situations. But, don't heed their unwise counsel. I can honestly say that God will not lead you into sin, just so He can glorify Himself by bringing you out of it. God does redeem us from the sins we've committed, but He doesn't tempt us to commit them.

So, if you are at the point of wanting to walk away this time—really, completely walk away—I encourage you to repent, which is to apologize to the Lord, ask for His forgiveness, receive it (He gives it freely, even if you don't *feel* forgiven yet), and take steps in your life in the direction opposite the relationship.

That last part is key. The relationship you were once feeding, you now need to starve. Stop making or taking those phone calls. No more e-mailing, texting, or chatting, and definitely no more in-person meetings with one another. And if you have a spouse, take steps toward reconciliation, inviting the Holy Spirit every step of the way. Also, cultivate a relationship with someone who can be your accountability partner. Having someone in your life to whom you are also accountable helps keep you going in the right direction. My accountability partner has been one of my greatest blessings.

This may sound difficult, and there will likely be a period when it feels difficult because of how much Satan doesn't want you freed from this. The amazing thing, though, is that as you do this and as the Holy Spirit works in and through you, you will be strengthened as life is poured into you rather than drained from you.

After ending your adulterous relationship, and before getting into another relationship, I urge you to take time to focus on healing. And if you're already married, intentionally focus on working towards and receiving healing for yourself and your marriage. Choose to forgive, and ask God to heal you of the wounds that adultery has inflicted on your heart and mind, including the ones you're not aware of but have great implications for the future.

There is no hurt within you that God can't heal, and I hope with all my heart that you know that. In His time and ways, He can heal you and—if you're single and marriage is in His plans for you—He can provide someone with whom you can cultivate a godly, covenant relationship. And it will be better than even the "best" day during the affair.

Single sisters, take the time now to focus on healing, preparation, and transformation for marriage. In fact, after a couple more years—and a few more dating disappointments—I reached a point of recognizing that I hadn't taken time to allow my Heavenly Father's love to heal me properly. I was still seeking various degrees of affirmation from the validation of men. So I decided to commit a full year to not dating. In fact, as I'm writing this, I am closing in on the tenth month; a little more than two months to go.

This is so much more than an act of abstinence, though. It is an immersion into more of who God is, and more of who He says I am. It is also not a starting and ending point, but a yearlong beginning. Many of our lifelong habits won't change overnight. I've been chronicling this journey in journals and a blog (www.theestheryear.blogspot.com), and plan to one day share the greatest and sweetest lessons learned from this year in another book. That time of healing is so important. And whether it is a year or a month, make sure that time is the amount of time God determines for you (not what you determine for God).

My prayer for you, whoever you are and wherever you are in life, is that you sense God's presence right now. I believe He has led you to this book for very specific purposes, and those purposes are good. He is right there with you, my friend and sister, right now. He's never left you this entire time, nor will He ever.

It's been my experience that when I feel like I can't see Him, it's because I've turned my back to Him, not the other way around. But that also just means He's standing right behind me, right there. He's there for you, too. You need only seek His face with all your heart, and you will see. You need only call on His name, and He will answer. Maybe not how or when you expect, but He will. He promises to, and He never breaks His promises.

10

Gratitude

As I begin this final chapter, I'm starting to cry. The idea of you reading this book is overwhelming right now. I still remember being that woman who was hugging her knees to her chest as she sat on the floor of her shower. If I could go back, I would hug her and hold her as she sobbed into my shirtsleeve. I would tell her the same thing I want to tell you before we part: God—*the Creator of the Universe*—loves you, loves you so much that He sent His only Son to Earth, and that only Son willingly went to the cross and was crucified and resurrected for you.

If you haven't already acknowledged His sacrifice and accepted Him as your Savior, He is really hoping you that will. I am, too, because there is no greater love in this world than the love He has for you. More than anything, I want you to experience that love.

I also want to tell you how grateful I am. I am so thankful you have invested time and care into reading about what God has done through this particular journey in my life. There was a point when I doubted I could ever write a book, let alone a book about this experience. There was a point in my life when I would have given almost anything to keep this part of my past a secret. To have gone from that point to the point of writing a book about that same part of my past is nothing short of a miracle. That's precisely what this has been for me, though: a miracle for which I thank God every day.

I hope as you close this book, God has used my story to open your heart to how He can redeem you and show His glory through your past, now and in the future. I hope you have a sense of great expectation for how God can—and wants to—work in and through your life. I hope you go forward feeling confident and free to speak the truth about your own life, sharing with other people who await the encouragement and hope you can bring to them.

I also hope you will join me in the mission to thwart whatever efforts Satan makes to ruin right relationships—right relationships between husbands and wives, and between God and us. Jesus died for each one of us to have redemption and right relationship with our Heavenly Father, from whom our sin had separated us.

Finally, I hope you know that even though your journey with me through this testimony is ending, the good that can happen with what God's revealed through it is just beginning.

My Prayer for You

First and foremost, Heavenly Father, thank You. Thank You for Your Son Jesus. Thank You for Your faithfulness, even when we are unfaithful. Thank You for how graciously and consistently You forgive us whenever we ask for forgiveness.

Jesus, thank You for willingly going to the cross so each and every one of us would have the opportunity to accept redemption. Thank You that because of Your sacrifice, we can have intimate relationships with You and God the Father, now and forever.

Jesus, I pray that all who read these words would know how much You love them. I pray they would know that You also died for them. If they do not know You as their Lord and Savior, I pray that You would soften their hearts. I pray they would know the truth, believing in their heart and confessing with their mouth that they are sinners, and believe that You are their Savior.

I pray for anyone at risk of committing adultery or currently committing adultery, Lord, that You would convict them of their sin. Convict them, while also pouring out a sense of Your redemptive mercy and forgiveness ready for them when they repent.

Please provide a glimpse of the good You have in store; provide a glimpse of Your power to restore relationships lost or broken in the process of their adultery. You have the power to reunite separated spouses; to heal the wounds from hurtful words and actions; to transform brokenness into beauty. You have the power to do anything and *everything* that is good—including what seems impossible to us.

Finally, Heavenly Father, show each and every one of us how we can better love You and each other. Teach us how we can each guard our hearts and protect covenant relationships—our own and others'. Revolutionize marriages. Bring revelation about how we can better respect and protect marriages; and *why* they need protection. And remind us of the fact that it is our joy to honor You—and it is for our benefit that You call us to abide by certain standards.

I love You, God. I love You, Jesus. And I am so thankful that You chose to use me in this way. I pray this testimony and every other testimony I give over the course of my life would be pleasing to You.

Amen.

About Rebecca

Words from the Other Woman is Rebecca's first book—but she hopes it won't be her last.

After graduating from Messiah College with a B.A. in English, Rebecca went on to work in state government; study International Policy and Conflict Resolution in Monterey, CA; and serve with one of the largest humanitarian organizations in the world.

Although she's lived in seven states and three countries (and counting), she's learned that home is wherever God has planted her. She currently resides near Seattle, WA, but enjoys finding reasons to explore other parts of the United States—and world. When she's not writing, she enjoys hiking, photography, pro-life and anti-human-trafficking advocacy, and fellowship with friends.

For more information about Rebecca and her writing (including future books), visit www.rebeccahalton.com.

About Meghan

After being in the same small group during summer internships at World Vision U.S., Rebecca knew she wanted Meghan's help and expertise when editing *Words from the Other Woman*. Rebecca was overjoyed to team with Meghan, and is very thankful for her professionalism and commitment to helping make this book the best it can be.

Meghan has a B.A. in English from Northwest University with a concentration in literature. Her internships with Thomas Nelson and World Vision have given her a chance to research, edit, and write for multiple formats.

Meghan lives in Seattle, WA. Because Seattle's propensity for rain often prevents long walks on the beach, she enjoys swing dancing instead.